The Griffin Poetry Prize Anthology

The Griffin Poetry Prize Anthology

A selection of the 2003 shortlist

Edited by Sharon Thesen

ANANSI

Published in 2003 by
House of Anansi Press Inc.
110 Spadina Avenue, Suite 801
Toronto, ON, M5V 2K4
Tel. 416-363-4343
Fax 416-363-1017
www.anansi.ca

Distributed in Canada by
Publishers Group Canada
250A Carlton Street
Toronto, ON, M5A 2L1
Tel. 416-934-9900
Toll free order numbers:
Tel. 800-663-5714
Fax 800-565-3770

The Griffin Trust logo used with permission

07 06 05 04 03   1 2 3 4 5

NATIONAL LIBRARY OF CANADA CATALOGUING IN PUBLICATION DATA

The Griffin poetry prize anthology : a selection of the 2003 shortlist /
edited and introduced by Sharon Thesen.

ISBN 0-88784-687-4

1. English poetry — 21st century. 2. Canadian poetry (English) — 21st century.
I. Thesen, Sharon, 1946–

PS8293.G6795 2003   821'.91408   C2003-900534-8
PR9195.7.G75 2003

Cover Design: Bill Douglas @ The Bang
Text Design: Tannice Goddard

THE CANADA COUNCIL | LE CONSEIL DES ARTS
FOR THE ARTS | DU CANADA
SINCE 1957 | DEPUIS 1957

*We acknowledge for their financial support of our publishing
program the Canada Council for the Arts, the Ontario Arts Council,
the Government of Ontario through the Ontario Media Development
Corporation's Ontario Book Initiative, and the Government of Canada
through the Book Publishing Industry Development Program (BPIDP).*

Printed and bound in Canada

CONTENTS

Preface, by Sharon Thesen   ix

International Finalists

Kathleen Jamie: *Mr and Mrs Scotland Are Dead*

Inhumation   5
Bosegran   6
God Almighty the First Garden Made   7
Arraheids   8
Child with Pillar Box and Bin Bags   9
Den of the Old Men   10
One of Us   12
Skeins o Geese   14

Paul Muldoon: *Moy Sand and Gravel*

The Misfits   17
Beagles   19
Winter Wheat   20
The Stoic   21
On   23
Eugenio Montale: *The Eel*   24
The Ancestor   25
Homesickness   26

Gerald Stern: *American Sonnets*

The Inkspots   29
Peaches   30
Mimi   31
All I Did For Him   32
Spider   33
Hats   34
Hydrangea   35
Large Pots   36
Samaritans   37
Roses   38

C. D. Wright: *Steal Away*

What No One Could Have Told Them   41
The Next to Last Draft   44
Song of the Gourd   46
Everything Good Between Men and Women   48
Ponds, in Love   49
Spring Street Girl Friend (#8)   50

Canadian Finalists

Margaret Avison: *Concrete and Wild Carrot*

Present from Ted   55
Ramsden   57
Balancing Out   58

The Whole Story   59
Cycle of Community   60
Prospecting   63

Dionne Brand: *thirsty*

I   67
II   69
III   71
IV   72
V   73
VI   74
VII   75

P. K. Page: *Planet Earth*

from Alphabetical   79
The Selves   85
The Metal and the Flower   86
Funeral Mass   87

About the Poets   89
Acknowledgements   93

To confer recognition of excellence in poetry upon only seven of the 350 or so poetry books published in English this year is to court sadness, turmoil, and often, terrible doubt. For are not all poetry books excellent — for a moment or two, a line or two, or even completely — in the mind of any given poet, publisher, reader, at any given time?

Such affectionate fancies, must, however, be jettisoned as the jury sorts through the books in search of seven that can withstand the adjective "excellent" without breaking apart. As David Young mentioned in his introduction to last year's *Griffin Poetry Prize Anthology*, the job of adjudicating this kind of competition "is not for the faint of heart." My co-jurors, the American poet Sharon Olds and the Irish poet Michael Longley, would agree that something happens during the deliberations that produces surprising results, results often quite different from what any one of us would have produced on our own. Many, many excellent books had to be put aside. Difficult decisions — such as choosing between a translation and an original work — had to be made. And in the end, given that consensus is a rare and complicated thing, we came up with a list of seven marvellous books.

The poets whose books comprise the two shortlists (Canadian and international) for the 2003 Griffin Poetry Prize have in common long experience in the art and craft of poetry. They also exemplify the alert, intelligent generosity that only poetry can extend to human experience, for both find their form and meaning in language. This year's books were on the whole lyrical and serious, dealing with elemental things: nature, mortality, love, grief — prescient, perhaps, of the kind of regrouping around a poetics of Eros that can occur at times of crisis and war. The books themselves were beautifully produced and printed; the publishers deserve credit for their work as well.

The selections from each of the shortlisted books in this anthology demonstrate the range and flexibility of poetic voice — diction that prefers, despite many temptations, the sovereignty of language to anything else, and which, at its best, evinces the uncanny ability to show reality to itself. The feeling of gratitude we experience in the presence of art is a clue to the truth of its particular and magical life, for nothing is quite as reviving, as miraculous, as a line of poetry. And good poems are made of good lines. Poetry, I believe, is one of the few antidotes we have to the toxicity of the plastic words of predation and management that have so colonized consciousness in our time. Poetry restores us to beauty and sanity, wildness and intelligence.

On behalf of Michael Longley, Sharon Olds, and myself: Many thanks to the Griffin Trust for making the 2003 Griffin Poetry Prize possible, for bringing poetry and readers together, for conferring honours upon at least some of the excellent poets in our midst who so deserve them.

— *Sharon Thesen*
Vancouver, April 2003

International Finalists

Kathleen Jamie

Mr and Mrs Scotland Are Dead: Poems 1980–1999

Kathleen Jamie appraises her roots while keeping an eye on far horizons. While there is of course much that is quintessentially Scottish in her poetry, her generous, transfiguring imagination takes in the world — Pakistan, Tibet, the Middle East as well as beloved native landscapes such as Orkney and Tayside. These poems are fleet in their chronicling and abundant in circumstantial detail, but also interior, spiritually entangled. Her humane vision brings to life the dangers of wartime and the peace of home. The edgy amorousness in some of the poems is matched by a chaste utterance that intensifies the erotic charge. She has perfect pitch, a natural sense of cadence and verbal melody that helps to give her work the feel of organic inevitability: her poems make their shapes as a fountain does (and the Jamie fountain is fed by pure springwater). The lovely surface-shimmer of her poetry beguiles us just as its inner radiance ensures that we will keep returning to it.

INHUMATION

No one knows if he opened his eyes,
acknowledged the dark,
felt around, found and drank
the mead provided, supposing
himself dead.

BOSEGRAN

Everything is natural, from the cotton summer
dress to the horizon; a natural illusion.
In the water of the cove, with its plates
of green weed fixed and shifting like continents,
is some irritation — an object discarded from a boat
or the few white houses on the shore
looking out to sea. The sea lies open as an eye.

Alone in all the world one is playing.
A seal, fluid and dark, has the plastic colonised,
round her like a jacket. I watched them tumble
and dive, and water cuff rock
till the sea took the colour of the sky. To what end?
— but 'why?' is just salt blown in the mind's eye.
The seal delights. The sun climbs higher as the world goes about.

GOD ALMIGHTY THE FIRST GARDEN MADE

How did I get where I am today?
How did I get where I am today? Lass,
I hauled mesel up by me own boot straps. See
all I started out with was seventeen jars of bluebells,
and were on funerals for years. Then I 'ad this idea . . .

For fenugreek, and marigolds, then along came the anemones,
down the mart at dawn, I bought in job lots of greenery,
expanded in a small way with a little blend for England
(hollyhocks and foxgloves and Cox's orange pippins).

Secured an export deal for cacti, but I got me fingers burned
on nettles. They'd no sooner got laburnum seeds
then they're clamouring for wheat. I gave it, too; albeit
with poppies. (I'm not a hard man, I hear deputations, Sundays.)

T'Word spread. Travellers went to Africa with suchlike
samples of exotica as malachite, antelopes, and a tropical strain
of thunder. Then t'was Lapsang Souchong and iridescent bees,
BUT I never forgot me roots, oh no! (Ah me! them Baobab trees!)

I'm getting on. I'll be calling it a day soon,
and handing over to me son. I just fidget
with hedgerows now, do a small line in peas. I like
to put me feet up on me footstool, sunny afternoons,
and cut me own toenails to meet demand for crescent moons.

ARRAHEIDS

See thon raws o flint arraheids
in oor gret museums o antiquities
awful grand in Embro —
Dae'ye near'n daur wunner at wur histrie?
Weel then, Bewaur!
The museums of Scotland are wrang.
They urnae arraheids
but a show o grannies' tongues,
the hard tongues o grannies
aa deid an guan
back to thur peat and burns,
but for thur sherp
chert tongues, that lee
fur generations in the land
like wicked cherms, that lee
aa douce in the glessy cases in the gloom
o oor museums, an
they arenae lettin oan. But if you daur
sorn aboot an fancy
the vanished hunter, the wise deer runnin on;
wheesht . . . an you'll hear them,
fur they cannae keep fae muttering
ye arenae here tae wonder,
whae dae ye think ye ur?

CHILD WITH PILLAR BOX AND BIN BAGS

But it was the shadowed street-side she chose
while Victor Gold the bookies basked
in conquered sunlight, and though
Dalry Road Licensed Grocer gloried and cast
fascinating shadows she chose
the side dark in the shade of tenements;
that corner where Universal Stores' (closed
for modernisation) blank hoarding blocked
her view as if that process were illegal;
she chose to photograph her baby here,
the corner with the pillar box.
In his buggy, which she swung to face her.
She took four steps back, but
the baby in his buggy rolled toward the kerb.
She crossed the ground in no time
it was fearful as Niagara,
she ran to put the brake on, and returned
to lift the camera, a cheap one.
The tenements of Caledonian Place neither
watched nor looked away, they are friendly buildings.
The traffic ground, the buildings shook, the baby breathed
and maybe gurgled at his mother as she
smiled to make him smile in his picture;
which she took on the kerb in the shadowed corner,
beside the post-box, under tenements, before
the bin-bags hot in the sun that shone
on them, on dogs, on people on the other side
the other side of the street to that she'd chosen,
if she'd chosen or thought it possible to choose.

C'mon ye auld buggers, one by one
this first spring day, slowly down
the back braes with your walking sticks
and wee brown dugs, saying: *Aye, lass*
a snell wind yet but braw. Ye
half dozen relics of strong men
sat in kitchen chairs
behind the green gingham curtain
of yer den, where a wee dog grins
on last year's calendar — we hear ye
clacking dominoes the afternoon for pennies.
And if some wee tyke
puts a chuckie through the window
ye stuff yesterday's Courier
in the broken pane, saying
jail's too guid fur them, tellies in cells!
        We can see your bunnets nod
and jaws move: what're ye up to
now you've your hut built,
now green hame-hammered benches
appear in the parish's secret soft-spots
like old men's spoor?
Is it carties? A tree-hoose?
Or will ye drag up driftwood;
and when she's busy with the bairns
remove your daughters' washing-lines
to lash a raft? Which,
if ye don't all fall out and argue
you can name the *Pride o' Tay* and launch
some bright blue morning on the ebb-tide

and sail away, the lot of yez,
staring straight ahead
          like captains
as you grow tiny
out on the wide Firth, tiny
as you drift past Ballinbriech, Balmurnie, Flisk
with your raincoats and bunnets,
          wee dugs and sticks.

We are come in a stone boat,
a miracle ship that steers itself
round skerries where guillemots
and shags stand still as graves.
Our sealskin cloaks are clasped
by a fist-sized penannular brooch,
our slippers are feathery
gugas' necks: so delicate
we carried them over the wracky shore,
past several rusted tractors. Truth:
this was a poor place, a
ragged land all worn to holes. No one,
nothing, but a distant
Telecom van, a bungalow
tied with fishing floats
for want of flowers.
                    That August night
the Perseid shower rained
on moor and lily-loch, on a frightened world —
on us, in a roofless shieling
with all our tat: the
golden horn of righteousness,
the justice harp; what folks expect.
We took swans' shape
to cross the Minch, one last fling
with silly magic — at our first
mainland steps a dormobile
slewed into a passing place; cameras flashed.

So we stayed high, surprised
a forester making aeolian flutes
from plastic tubes,
he shared his pay. 'Avoid
the A9. For God's sake,
get some proper clothes.' We ditched
the cloaks, bought yellow
Pringle sweaters in Spean Bridge,
and house by safe house
arrived in Edinburgh. So far so
tedious: we all hold
minor government jobs, lay plans, and bide our time.

SKEINS O GEESE

Skeins o geese write a word
across the sky. A word
struck lik a gong
afore I wis born.
The sky moves like cattle, lowin.

I'm as empty as stane, as fields
ploo'd but not sown, naked
an blin as a stane. Blin
tae the word, blin
tae a' soon but geese ca'ing.

Wire twists lik archaic script
roon a gate. The barbs
sign tae the wind as though
it was deef. The word whustles
ower high for ma senses. Awa.

No lik the past which lies
strewn aroun. Nor sudden death.
No like a lover we'll ken
an connect wi forever.
The hem of its goin drags across the sky.

Whit dae birds write on the dusk?
A word niver spoken or read.
The skeins turn hame,
on the wind's dumb moan, a soun,
maybe human, bereft.

Paul Muldoon

Moy Sand and Gravel

Reading Paul Muldoon's poetry is like looking through a kaleidoscope while he jiggles your elbow. The complex rhyme-schemes, the repeated words and phrases, the refrains, the wonderful patterning unexpectedly dislocate this poet's deep sense of place and shuttle the reader between order and chaos and back again. He reminds us that rhyme used with great resource does not restrain: rather, it is aleatory; it beckons the random and the risky. It is indeed a rich paradox that this most à la mode of poets takes us right back, again and again, to poetry's ancient beginnings. As well as leading us a merry dance, he tells stories and sings cradlesongs and makes up nursery rhymes and riddles and says prayers. His elegies and love poems are among the finest of our times. With Mozartian grace and daring he renovates the traditional forms — sestina, sonnet, haiku. In modernizing the time-honoured he keeps surprising himself and his readers.

THE MISFITS

If and when I did look up, the sky over the Moy was the very same
                                        gray-blue
as the slow lift
of steam-smoke over the seam
of manure on a midwinter morning. I noticed the splash of red lead
on my left boot as again and again I would bend
my knee and bury my head in the rich

black earth the way an ostrich
was rumored to bury its head. My hands were blue
with cold. Again and again I would bend
to my left and lift
by one handle a creel of potatoes — King Edwards, gray as lead —
mined from what would surely seem

to any nine- or ten-year-old an inexhaustible seam.
My father wore a bag-apron that read, in capital letters, RICH.
My own capital idea, meanwhile, had sunk like a lead
balloon. "Blow all you like," my father turned on me. "Talk till you're blue
in the face. I won't let you take a lift
from the Monk. Blow all you like. I won't bend."

The Monk had spent twenty-odd years as a priest in South Bend,
his face priest-smooth except for a deep seam
in his left cheek. Fred Grew said something strange about how he liked to
                                        "lift
his shirttail." Jack Grimley chipped in with how he was "ostrich-
sized" because he once lent Joe Corr a book called *Little Boy Blue*.
When Fred Grew remarked on his having "no lead

in his pencil," I heard myself say, cool as cool, "I think you've all been
>misled."
At which the RICHARDSON'S TWO-SWARD suddenly began to unbend
in that distinctive pale blue
lettering as the seam
of his bag-apron unstitched itself and my father turned on me again:
>"That's rich,
all right. If you think, after that, I'd let the Monk give you a lift

into the Moy to see Montgomery bloody Clift
you've another think coming. I'll give him two barrels full of twelve-gauge
>lead
if he comes anywhere near you. Bloody popinjay. Peacock. *Ostrich*."
All I could think of was how the Monk was now no more likely to show me
>how to bend

that note on the guitar — "like opening a seam
straight into your heart" — when he played Bessie Smith's "Cold in Hand
>Blues"

than an ostrich to bend
its lead-plumed wings and, with its two-toed foot, rip out the horizon seam
and lift off, somehow, into the blue.

BEAGLES

That Boxing Day morning, I would hear the familiar, far-off gowls and
          gulders
over Keenaghan and Aughanlig
of a pack of beagles, old dogs disinclined to chase a car suddenly quite
          unlike
themselves, pups coming helter-skelter
across the plowlands with all the chutzpah of veterans
of the trenches, their slate-grays, cinnamons, liver-browns, lemons, rusts,
         and violets
turning and twisting, unseen, across the fields,
their gowls and gulders turning and twisting after the twists and turns
of the great hare who had just now sauntered into the yard where I stood
         on tiptoe
astride my new Raleigh cycle,
his demeanor somewhat louche, somewhat lackadaisical
under the circumstances, what with him standing on tiptoe
as if to mimic me, standing almost as tall as I, looking as if he might for a
         moment put
himself in my place, thinking better of it, sloping off behind the lorry bed.

WINTER WHEAT

I

The plowboy was something his something as I nibbled the lobe
of her right ear and something her blouse
for the Empire-blotchy globe
of her left breast on which there something a something louse.

II

Those something lice like something seed pearls
and her collar something with dandruff
as when Queen Elizabeth entertained the Earls
in her something something ruff.

III

I might have something the something groan
of the something plowboy who would with such something urge
the something horses, a something and a roan,

had it not been for the something splurge
of something like the hare
which even now managed to something itself from the something
                                        plowshare.

THE STOIC

This was more like it, looking up to find a burlapped fawn
halfway across the iced-over canal, an Irish navvy who'd stood there for an
age
with his long-tailed shovel or broad griffawn,
whichever foot he dug with showing the bandage

that saved some wear and tear, though not so much that there wasn't a leak
of blood through the linen rag, a red picked up nicely by the turban
he sported, those reds lending a little brilliance to the bleak
scene of suburban or — let's face it — *urban*

sprawl, a very little brilliance. This was more like the afternoon last March
when I got your call in St. Louis and, rather than rave
as one might rant and rave at the thought of the yew
from Deirdre's not quite connecting with the yew from Naoise's grave,

rather than shudder like a bow of yew or the matchless Osage orange
at the thought of our child already lost from view
before it had quite come into range,
I steadied myself under the Gateway Arch

and squinted back, first of all, through an eyelet of bone
to a point where the Souris
had not as yet hooked up with the Assiniboine,
to where the Missouri

had not as yet been swollen by the Osage,
then ahead to where — let's face it — there are now *two* fawns
on the iced-over canal, two Irish navvies who've stood there for a veritable

                                                                          age

with their long-tailed shovels or broad griffawns.

ON

Absalom was riding his mule and the mule passed under the thick branches of a great oak. Absalom's head got caught in the oak and he was left hanging between heaven and earth, while the mule he was riding went on.

— II SAMUEL 18:9

I make my way alone through the hand-to-hand fighting
to A3 and A5. Red velvet. Brass and oak.
The special effects will include strobe lighting
and artificial smoke.

A glance to A5. Patrons are reminded, *mar bheadh*,
that the management accepts no responsibility in the case of theft.
Even as the twenty-five-piece orchestra
that's masked offstage left

strikes up, there's still a chance, I suppose, that the gainsayers
might themselves be gainsaid
as you rush, breathless, into my field of vision.

Understudies and standbys never substitute for listed players,
however, unless a specific announcement is made.
There will be no intermission.

EUGENIO MONTALE: *THE EEL*

The selfsame, the siren
of icy waters, shrugging off as she does the Baltic
to hang out in our seas,
our inlets, the rivers
through which she climbs, bed-hugger, who keeps going against
the flow, from branch to branch, then
from capillary to snagged capillary,
farther and farther in, deeper and deeper into the heart
of the rock, straining
through mud runnels, till one day
a flash of light from the chestnut trees
sends a fizzle through a standing well,
through a drain that goes
by dips and darts from the Apennines to the Romagna —
the selfsame eel, a firebrand now, a scourge,
the arrow shaft of Love on earth
which only the gulches or dried-out
gullies of the Pyrenees might fetch and ferry back
to some green and pleasant spawning ground,
a green soul scouting and scanning
for life where only
drought and desolation have hitherto clamped down,
the spark announcing
that all sets forth when all that's set forth
is a charred thing, a buried stump,
this short-lived rainbow, its twin met
in what's set there between your eyelashes,
you who keep glowing as you do, undiminished, among the sons
of man, faces glistening with your slime, can't you take in
her being your next-of-kin?

THE ANCESTOR

The great-grandmother who bears down on us, as if beholding the mote
in our eye, from a nineteenth-century Hungarian portrait
on our library wall is no relation. Not even remote.
The straw-hatted man in a daguerreotype, though he and I may share the
trait

of putting two fingers to the little carbuncle
on our right chin, is no more of my blood than I am
consanguineous with Cromwell. Our Webster's is inscribed "Philip. Best
uncle."
Our napkins bear an unfamiliar monogram.

Yet how familiar all become. Shaving mug, gymkhana rosette, five charms
from a charm bracelet — all those heirlooms
to which we're now the heirs are at once more presentable and

more present than our own. This great-grandmother with folded arms
who lurches and looms
across the library may not be so unreasoning in her reprimand.

HOMESICKNESS

The lion stretched like a sandstone lion on the sandstone slab
of a bridge with one fixture, a gaslight,
looks up from his nicotine-worried forepaw
with the very same air my father, Patrick,
had when the results came back from the lab,
that air of anguish-awe
that comes with the realization of just how slight
the chances are of anything doing the trick

as the sun goes down over Ballyknick and Ballymacnab
and a black-winged angel takes flight.

The black-winged angel leaning over the sandstone parapet
of the bridge wears a business suit, dark gray.
His hair is slick with pomade.
He turns away as my mother, Brigid,
turned away from not only her sandstone pet
but any concession being made.
The black-winged angel sets her face to the unbending last ray
of evening and meets rigid with rigid

as the sun goes down over Lisnagat and Listamlet
and Clonmore and Clintyclay.

Gerald Stern

American Sonnets: Poems

Gerald Stern's poems are astonishing; they have profound suppleness, tenderness, and power. When we finish one of these American sonnets, we laugh or cry out loud, incredulous. Each one seems to begin in pure freedom, then the last line, like a magnet, turns out to have been pulling the whole poem toward itself with the momentum of history and eros. The work is both intimate and inclusive, and the implied reader seems to be unusually present to the speaker's spirit! The poems are alive with passion and with ironic energy, an irony so in love with the earth it seems to need a new name — milk and honey irony — and yet the tragic knowledge of the world here is hard as iron. This is the great art of a fierce mourning ecstatic, whose genius nourishes us.

THE INKSPOTS

The thing about the dove was how he cried in
my pocket and stuck his nose out just enough to
breathe some air and get some snow in his eye and
he would have snuggled in but I was afraid
and brought him into the house so he could shit on
the *New York Times*, still I had to kiss him
after a minute, I put my lips to his beak
and he knew what he was doing, he stretched his neck
and touched me with his open mouth, lifting
his wings a little and readjusting his legs,
loving his own prettiness, and I just
sang from one of my stupid songs from one of my
vile decades, the way I do, I have to
admit it was something from *trains*. I knew he'd like that,
resting in the coal car, slightly dusted with
mountain snow, somewhere near Altoona,
the horseshoe curve he knew so well, his own
moan matching the train's, a radio
playing the Inkspots, the engineer roaring.

PEACHES

What was I thinking of when I threw one of my
peach stones over the fence at Metro North,
and didn't I dream as always it would take
root in spite of the gravel and the newspaper,
and wasn't I like that all my life, and who isn't?
I thought of oranges and, later, watermelon
and yellow mangoes hanging from sweetened strings,
but it was peaches, wasn't it, peaches most of
all I thought about and if the two trees that
bore such hard little fruit would only have lived
a few years more how I would have had a sister
and I would have watched her blossom, her brown curls
her blue eyes, though given her family she would have
been wild and stubborn, harsh maybe, she would
be the angry one — how quiet I was — the Chinese
grew their peaches for immortality — the
Russians planted theirs so they could combine
beauty and productivity, that was
my aesthetic too, I boiled my grape leaves,
I ate my fallen apples, loving sister.

MIMI

I had to see *La Bohème* again just to
make sure for there was a little part of
me that kept the regret though when I tried
the argument again I used both hands
in order to explain and I was especially
sensitive to the landlord for I lived
both inside and outside even when I was angry
I paid my debts for I have listened to
and lived with grasshoppers and they bore me, but
Mimi, Mimi, when your hand dropped every
woman in my row was weeping and I
gave in too instead of gripping the armrest
or rubbing the back of my head; I loved it the most that
you lived inside and outside too, the snowdrop
was what you thought of, wasn't it? You were
the one who came back, three times, it was your stubbornness,
your loyalty. One time I stood in the street
and watched a moon so thin the clouds went through it
as if there were no body, as if the cold
was so relentless nothing could live there, you with
the blackened candle, you who stitched the lily.

ALL I DID FOR HIM

When I fought the dog we almost danced
we loved each other that much and he was strong,
not counting even his teeth and claws, and I had
trouble pushing against him even though his
shoulders were weaker in that position nor was he
intended, as Aristotle might say, for fighting
standing up like that the way maybe a
bear was more intended or certainly an
ape with his gross imitation of a
human, or a human of him, if I can
step into that muck a minute, and he was
taller than me, as I remember, which made him
huge for a dog and made me feel small standing
on two legs with my weak left knee impaired
as it was and smelling his breath and shocked by his giant
head and what had to be a look I never
expected in his eyes, though I had to know
it would be like that for who was I anyhow
to bicker as I did or think that love
as I called it, all I did for him, the food
and water I gave him I could barter, I couldn't
even find my pocket, I couldn't take out a dollar.

SPIDER

How you like these threads, said white spider
traveling back and forth between two rooms in
Lambertville, New Jersey, his web a work of
art, truly excessive, spit from his soul,
and the first case of any spit, it came from
my own soul since I am a mimic neurotic.
But how you like my steel? You like my window?
You like my big eye waiting? How you like my
chandelier? How you like fate? You like
my silk? Do cover your legs, do tighten
the arms a little, do tighten around the neck.
And how you like my kiss? How about
my rasping bloody tongue? Weren't those herbs
and such like any household, giant unkempt
Russian sage, the better to smell you, my dear,
and spicy rosemary beside the orange and
purple echinacea, all that a little
to placate — though I know you don't believe it,
for nature is nature — your perverted Isaiah
from running around like crazy in the meat markets.

HATS

For the sake of the fleabane growing rose a little
in the white to give it a natural look, almost
a tree with the branches going left and right and
leaves in the lower limbs, the center golden
and fecund there at the side of the yard as if to
apologize, the petals, if those are petals,
thin as threads, I touch my cream-colored hat;
and for the sake of the hat itself, since hats
are holy to any unreformed Jew, I stand
in front of the single rose of Sharon the deer
ignore — as far as eating — and extend
my hand to the blossoms and thank them for their time —
by folding and crushing my hat, my wrists spread out on
my chest, by pushing the brim to the top of my brow
as if I were sweating, by putting the hat on sideways,
then backwards, then with my right hand touching the rear
ribbon and tilting the peak downward, then taking
the crease out — like a derby, then pulling it down
almost to my ears, all this to thank them
for blooming over and over, for not disappearing.

HYDRANGEA

I was pleased by blue hydrangea because at
last I had a flower from a gorgeous
family I could hate just as when certain
say Jewish poets, whom I'm supposed to revere
because they're Jewish and not to love them would be
an act of betrayal to all eleven prophets;
dozens of kings and clothing manufacturers;
dentists, chess players, swimmers, stockbrokers, English teachers;
psychiatrists, painters, physicists, salesmen, violinists;
social workers, merchants, lawyers, cutters, trimmers;
critics; reveal themselves as snobs and bigots
and analytical and anti-passionate which could be
for all I know another side of Judaism
since Judaism has three sides as in the
Mercy, as in the Exceptions, as in the Melancholies,
which takes me back to the blue hydrangea I see
between an opening in the fence, it looks like
the blue was painted on, I hate it, I also
hate the red carnation, I love the cream
and when it's cone-shaped, I even like the pink,
may God forgive me, Lord of the lost and destitute.

LARGE POTS

It's like coming through a chrysanthemum forest
and one of the pots had swollen grapes painted on
and leaves the size of hands, and one had a bird,
and one had a geometric design at first I thought
were Cretan dancers and athletes walking into
a kind of stadium and all together the colors were
reds and golds; specifically they are pink
and perfect rust and perfect orange and they are
starting to turn to straw although it's only
the tenth of October, my former wife's birthday,
one of only five I know including my
own in February. I started to turn to straw
maybe a year ago, maybe less, with humans
it's more complex, it's not a question of dryness
only, but what do I know? I walk from
pot to pot, I walk from straw man to straw man,
I kiss them goodbye, I know I surprise them, *most* people
juke a little when you kiss them, I kiss
mahogany man goodbye, I kiss his wife,
a coral rose, I hold her for nine or ten seconds.

SAMARITANS

I can't remember what the class trip was —
I think we were going to visit the Samaritans
who lived in round houses at the border of
West Virginia. They believed in a round eye
staring at God, or maybe it was God who had
the eye and stared at them and Moses alone was
the light, as far as they were concerned, and his was
the only law they followed, forget the other
prophets, so-called; and how they got to West Virginia
I forget, though I know our teacher, a specialist
in sociology, was teaching religion
when we went on the trip. I think I got
waylaid a little, the way you did then:
it was spring and warm, the girls had on
light dresses and we had cigarettes, the chimney
holes looked like eyes, but it was God's eye
that I will never forget, it followed the bus
back to Pittsburgh and sometimes it seemed to smile
the way an eye smiles though it was incorporeal
of course and my own eyes were closed — I was sleeping.

ROSES

There was a rose called Guy de Maupassant,
a carmine pink that smelled like a Granny Smith
and there was another from the seventeenth century
that wept too much and wilted when you looked;
and one that caused tuberculosis, doctors
dug them up, they wore white masks and posted
warnings in the windows. One wet day
it started to hail and pellets the size of snowballs
fell on the roses. It's hard for me to look at
a Duchess of Windsor, it was worn by Franco
and Mussolini, it stabbed Jews; yesterday I bought
six roses from a Haitian on Lower Broadway;
he wrapped them in blue tissue paper, it was
starting to snow and both of us had on the wrong shoes,
though it was wind, he said, not snow that ruined
roses and all you had to do was hold them
against your chest. He had a ring on his pinky
the size of a grape and half his teeth were gone.
So I loved him and spoke to him in false Creole
for which he hugged me and enveloped me
in his camel hair coat with most of the buttons missing,
and we were brothers for life, we swore it in French.

C. D. Wright

Steal Away: Selected and New Poems

C. D. Wright's work is plain gorgeous; it is clean-wrought, rich, rambunctious, and pure-thrown, like a perfect game. This is the generous art of a graceful outlaw troubadour, singing to us as if from within ourselves. The poems seem written not with ink or pencil-lead but with life-stuff itself as their matter, alphabet, and orthography. They are dense with a sense of substance and absence, love and grief and humour and horror. And how unusual it is, this mix of classes, races, sensualities, economies, and vocabularies — as if a people were writing its (our) true poetry. Here is a radical home voice, an original vision, luminously peculiar/precise; here is a new American music, with a green, wisdom-struck clarity and mercy.

Once he comes to live on the outside of her, he will not sleep
through the night or the next 400. He sleeps not, they sleep not.
Ergo they steer gradually mad. The dog's head shifts another
paw under the desk. Over a period of 400 nights.

You will see, she warns him. Life is full of television sets,
invoices, organs of other animals thawing on counters.

In her first dream of him, she leaves him sleeping on Mamo's
salt-bag quilt behind her alma mater. Leaves him to the Golden
Goblins. Sleep, pretty one, sleep.

. . . *the quilt that comforted her brother's youthful bed, the*
quilt he took to band camp.

Huh oh, he says, Huh oh. His word for many months.
Merrily pouring a bottle of Pledge over the dog's dull coat. And
with a round little belly that shakes like jelly.

Waiting out a shower in the Border Cafe; the bartender
spoons a frozen strawberry into his palm-leaf basket while they
lift their frosted mugs in a grateful click.

He sits up tall in his grandfather's lap, waving and waving to
the Blue Bonnet truck. Bye, blue, bye.

In the next dream he stands on his toes, executes a flawless
flip onto the braided rug. Resprings to crib.

*The salt-bag quilt goes everywhere, the one the bitch
Rosemary bore her litters on. The one they wrap around the
mower, and bundle with black oak leaves.*

How the bowl of Quick Quaker Oats fits his head.

He will have her milk at 1:42, 3:26, 4 a.m. Again at 6. Bent
over the rail to settle his battling limbs down for an afternoon
nap. Eyes shut, trying to picture what in the world she has on.

His nightlight — a snow-white pair of porcelain owls.

They remember him toothless, with one tooth, two tooths,
five or seven scattered around in his head. They can see the day
when he throws open his jaw to display several vicious rows.

Naked in a splash of sun, he pees into a paper plate the guest
set down in the grass as she reached for potato chips.

Suppertime, the dog takes leave of the desk's cool cavity to
patrol his highchair.

How patiently he pulls Kleenex from a box. Tissue by tissue.
How quietly he stands at the door trailing the White Cloud;
swabs his young hair with the toilet brush.

*The dog inherits the salt-bag quilt. The one her Mamo made
when she was seventeen — girlfriends stationed around a frame in black stockings
sewing, talking about things their children would do;*

He says: cereal, byebye, shoe, raisin, nobody. He hums.

She stands before the medicine chest, drawn. Swiftly he tumps discarded Tampax and hair from an old comb into her tub.

Wearily the man enters the house through the back. She isn't dressed. At the table there is weeping. Curses. Forking dried breasts of chicken.

while Little Sneed sat on the floor beneath the frame, pushing the needles back through.

One yawn followed by another yawn. Then little fists screwing little eyes. The wooden crib stuffed with bears and windup pillows wheeled in to receive him. Out in a twinkle. The powdered bottom airing the dark. The 400th night. When they give up their last honeyed morsel of love; the dog nestles in the batting of the salt-bag quilt commencing its long mope unto death.

More years pass and the book does not leave the drawer.
According to our author the book does not begin but opens on
a typewriter near a radiator. The typing machine has been
aimed at the window overlooking a park. It's been oiled and
blown out. At heart it is domestic as an old washer with the
white sheets coming off the platen. In the missing teeth much
has been suppressed. In the space and a half, regrettable things
have been said. Nothing can be taken back. The author wanted
this book to be friendly, to say, Come up on the porch with
me, I've got peaches; I don't mind if you smoke. It would be
written in the author's own voice. A dedication was planned to
Tyrone and Tina whose names the author read in a sidewalk on
Broad. The machine's vocation was to type, but its avocation
was to tell everyone up before light, I love you, I always will; to
tell the sisters waiting on their amniocenteses, Everything's
going to be fine. And to make something happen for the
hundreds of Floridians betting the quinella. It would have
dinner ready for people on their feet twelve hours a day. And
something else for the ones making bread hand over fist, the
gouging s-o-bs. But the book was too dependent. Women were
scattered across pages who loved the desert, but moved into
town to meet a man. The women, understand, weren't getting
any younger. Some of these women were pecking notes into the
text when the author was out walking. One note said: John Lee
you're still in my dreambooks, et cetera. The author had no
foresight. In previous drafts the good died right off like notes
on an acoustic guitar. Others died of money, that is, fell of
odorless, invisible, utterly quiet wounds. The work recorded

whatever it heard: dog gnawing its rump, the stove's clock, man next door taking out his cans, and things that went on farther down, below buildings and composts, all with the patience of a dumb beast chewing grass, with the inconsolable eyes of the herd. Basically the book was intended as a hair-raising document of the organisms. Thus and so the book opens: I have been meaning to write you for a long long time. I've been feeling so blue John Lee.

In gardening I continued to sit on my side of the car: to
drive whenever possible at the usual level of distraction:
in gardening I shat nails glass contaminated dirt and
threw up on the new shoots: in gardening I learned to
praise things I had dreaded: I pushed the hair out of my
face: I felt less responsible for one man's death one
woman's long-term isolation: my bones softened: in
gardening I lost nickels and ring settings I uncovered
buttons and marbles: I laid half the worm aside and
sought the rest: I sought myself in the bucket and won-
dered why I came into being in the first place: in gar-
dening I turned away from the television and went
around smelling of offal the inedible parts of the
chicken: in gardening I said excelsior: in gardening I re-
quired no company I had to forgive my own failure to
perceive how things were: I went out barelegged at
dusk and dug and dug and dug: I hit rock my ovaries
softened: in gardening I was protean as in no other
realm before or since: I longed to torch my old belong-
ings and belch a little flame of satisfaction: in gardening
I longed to stroll farther into soundlessness: I could al-
most forget what happened many swift years ago in
arkansas: I felt like a god from down under: chthonian:
in gardening I thought this is it body and soul I am
home at last: excelsior: praise the grass: in gardening I
fled the fold that supported the war: only in gardening
could I stop shrieking: stop: stop the slaughter: only in
gardening could I press my ear to the ground to hear
my soul let out an unyielding noise: my lines softened: I

turned the water onto the joy-filled boychild: only in
gardening did I feel fit to partake to go on trembling in
the last light: I confess the abject urge to weed your
beds while the bittersweet overwhelmed my daylilies: I
summoned the courage to grin: I climbed the hill with
my bucket and slept like a dipper in the cool of your
body: besotted with growth; shot through by green

has been written in mud and butter
and barbecue sauce. The walls and
the floors used to be gorgeous.
The socks off-white and a near match.
The quince with fire blight
but we get two pints of jelly
in the end. Long walks strengthen
the back. You with a fever blister
and myself with a sty. Eyes
have we and we are forever prey
to each other's teeth. The torrents
go over us. Thunder has not harmed
anyone we know. The river coursing
through us is dirty and deep. The left
hand protects the rhythm. Watch
your head. No fires should be
unattended. Especially when wind. Each
receives a free swiss army knife.
The first few tongues are clearly
preparatory. The impression
made by yours I carry to my grave. It is
just so sad so creepy so beautiful.
Bless it. We have so little time
to learn, so much . . . The river
courses dirty and deep. Cover the lettuce.
Call it a night. O soul. Flow on. Instead.

PONDS, IN LOVE

One was always going when the other was coming back
One was biting a green apple
The deeper the evening the louder the singing
Throwing the core out the window
An oar stirred the dark and then quit
A face drenches itself in carlight
A wrist wearing a man's watch dipped a net
Even as one turned toward an unfinished building
The other wondered what one would have on
Upon returning will the hair be fallen or cropped
If one reaches what is grasped for
Gnats go for the eyes
Will utter disappointment set in
Will it be water or milk or wine tonight
Mostly one listened in the low-intensity glow
Of events one sustains incomprehensible feelings

SPRING STREET GIRL FRIEND (#8)

In the snug harbors, helicopter and electric eel
blink like stringlight in the pathetic, exhaust-resistant trees.
There has to be one more night like this, and then
peace and prosperity will reign for an even minute.
The vendor's hands don't look very clean, but we knew
it was a dirty city. The chestnuts smell deceptively good; we're
hungry even though they are mealy, and then
she comes down in her otis elevator holding a cricket cage.
She purposely wears the purple terrycloth robe of nobility.
The music scarcely changes up until now, and then
with the tiniest monogrammed scissors we snip
a ribbon of undergraduate hair.
She offers the food of her breasts.
She does not give a fig about our depression
glass; she's not into collectibles.
She does not rust or crack; up to this point
we know no more than two of the names under which she wrote
nor her intellectual milieu. The buddha
in the takeout emanates an unknown strain of mercy,
and then we get suddenly scared and tell the driver
we want transfers to the real world
where the fish smell like fish and the cheese like cheese.

Canadian Finalists

Margaret Avison

Concrete and Wild Carrot

If beauty, as Alfred North Whitehead defines it, is "a quality which finds its exemplification in actual occasions," and if beauty is more completely exemplified in "imperfection and discord" than in the "perfection of harmony," then Margaret Avison's *Concrete and Wild Carrot* is an occasion of beauty. Avison's poetry is also alive in its sublimity and its humility: "wonder, readiness, simplicity" — the gifts of perception Avison attributes to her Christian faith — imbue every poem in this book with a rare spirit of disorderly love. Margaret Avison is a national treasure. For many decades she has forged a way to write, against the grain, some of the most humane, sweet, and profound poetry of our time.

PRESENT FROM TED

It must have been after a
birthday; at Christmastime
daylight hasn't the lambency
I remember as part of
the puzzling present somebody
had given me: a scribbler, empty pages, but
not for scribbling in.
Instead of a pencil box there was
a jellyglass set out, with water, and
a brand-new paint brush.

The paper was not pretty.
A pencil-point might in an upstroke
accidentally jab a hole in it.

But, painting it —
as I was told to, with only
clear water, "Behold!"
my whole being sang out, for "see"
would not have been adequate.

The pictures that emerged
were outlines? I remember
only the paper, and the wonder of it,
and how each page was turning out to be
a different picture.

There were no colours, were there?

In the analogy, there are
glorious colours
and, in some way that lacks
equivalents,
deepening colours, patterns that keep
emerging, always
more to anticipate.

For that there is no other process.

Locked in the picture is
missing the quality of the analogy of
morning light
and the delighted holder of the paint-brush
and who gave him the book, and where he found it.

RAMSDEN

Let's go to the park where
the dogs and children
cluster and circle and run
under the sombre old trees — they are
hanging on to their swarthing
leaves — while the young
medallioned trees in the early
sun are dancing
among them.
The knapsacked students too
hurtle, always too late, focused
on there, blindingly
swerving out of the now and
here where children and dogs
and a few rather shabby, slow
old ones, straying, move
across the owners, standing with
loose leashes, intent on "their day."
The benched but sleepless
mothers and nannies, watching,
are quieted here, warmed and fed
by the good old trees and
the shining little ones.

BALANCING OUT

He smells of — what?
It's like wet coal-dust.
He came very late:
tangled brown hair, his face
streaked, and bleary;
no gloves, but (Merry
Christmas) from a mission, twice
blest — a good warm coat
that could go anywhere — and had!
now puckered, snagged, hem spread
from sleeping out, and ripped
around one leather elbow,
and buttoned crooked. There were no
other buttons now. He slept
there in his pew.

The giver of his topcoat eerily
watched, her widow's desolation clearly
inconsolable now
(a pang — like joy!),
to see what she had seen
on a fine, and steady man
made come full circle on this ruined fellow.

Still, he had his coat,
and she, the echoing years.

THE WHOLE STORY

Behind that stone before
it was rolled away
a corpse lay.
There lay all I deplore:
fear, truculence — much more
that to any other I need not say.
But behind that stone I must be sure
of deadness, to allay
self-doubt, i.e. so nearly to ignore
the love and sacrifice for our
release; to nearly stray
back into the old
pursuit of virtue.

Once it is clear
it was a corpse that day,
then, then, we know the glory
of the clean place, the floor
of rock, those linens, know the hour
of His inexplicable "Peace;" the pour
— after He went away —
of wonder, readiness, simplicity,
given.

CYCLE OF COMMUNITY

Mid-morning paraffin film over the
dayshine has
incidentally opened the ear
to little clanks and whirrs
out there, the hum
of a world going on,
untroubled by the silent witness, sky.
We here are silent. Yet being
drawn into, with, each
creature, each machine-work
thump, each step, faraway bark,
buzz, whine, rustle, etc.
goes to give our city
a voice, dampered by distance;
serves, through outer
windless openness of skywash, to
open a bud of tremulous hearing.

Full day will blare away
later. Then —
walk (an even pace) where cars, trucks, a
cement-mixer, teenagers out of school,
and a tied puppy keening
outside the grocer's,
provide a mix the studios would
take pride in.

Go steadily for your sake and
the others' on the sidewalk
burrowing by. And keep your face
like anyone's, in
pedestrious preoccupation —
although
you'll have to part your lips
a little, to play in.
First, test the pitch of the
prevailing din
(humming), then (still with no
perceptible opening of the mouth)
intone on the same tone-level
with all the enveloping street-sound.
Louder. As loudly as you can!

Nobody hears a thing,
                              even yourself!
Otherwise surely someone would
give that quick glance of
furtive avoidance that flicks
some flushed and angrily
gesturing man you may
hear shouting along
anywhere about town. He chooses

to stray apart from the
condemnable crazy world.

Surprisingly, evening, after the hours
of sharp light, closes in
overcast. Our thunderous busynesses
shift into calmer surge and flow.
Before dark (sky and windows
contemplating emptiness) we half-
hear the foghorn and remember
the lake, and night.

PROSPECTING

There is a node. There, one day,
all ways will
swiftly converge.

      Evening's, or morning-
      star glimmers from dear old —
      too old now — burlap earth-skies.

      Behold the abandoned
      once historied
      home of us people.

Our present
orbital rush singles out some
veering.
Plumblines occur.

      (Abandoned? no,
      not yet quite smouldered out within
      a few of us.)

All waves
(once ear and eye and intuition's

and science's) wash into
symphonic silence.

Time, too.
For at the node
all energies become
that unrewarded effortless and
ruthless kindness,
Person.

Dionne Brand

thirsty

The word "thirsty" in Dionne Brand's long poem is a dying man's last utterance. Shot by the police in his own front yard, Alan is a Christie Pits Jeremiah as well as a tender nurturer of plants, an immigrant and a dreamer who thirsts for "a calming loving spot" among the "conditional places" and "conditional sentences" that perpetuate the marginalization of the poor. *Thirsty* is a reckoning with the pretenses of community in the soul-withering environments of today's mega-cities. But Brand's luscious and ferocious lines go beyond a critique of dystopian realities to construct, in themselves, in their keen, lyric intelligence, an oasis of truth, compassion, and sensuality.

I

This city is beauty
unbreakable and amorous as eyelids,
in the streets, pressed with fierce departures,
submerged landings,
I am innocent as thresholds
and smashed night birds, lovesick,
as empty elevators

let me declare doorways,
corners, pursuit, let me say
standing here in eyelashes, in
invisible breasts, in the shrinking lake
in the tiny shops of untrue recollections,
the brittle, gnawed life we live,
I am held, and held

the touch of everything blushes me,
pigeons and wrecked boys,
half-dead hours, blind musicians,
inconclusive women in bruised dresses
even the habitual grey-suited men with terrible
briefcases, how come, how come
I anticipate nothing as intimate as history

would I have had a different life
failing this embrace with broken things,
iridescent veins, ecstatic bullets, small cracks

in the brain, would I know these particular facts,
how a phrase scars a cheek, how water
dries love out, this, a thought as casual
as any second eviscerates a breath

and this, we meet in careless intervals,
in coffee bars, gas stations, in prosthetic
conversations, lotteries, untranslatable
mouths, in versions of what we may be,
a tremor of the hand in the realization
of endings, a glancing blow of tears
on skin, the keen dismissal in speed

II

There was a Sunday morning scent,
an early morning air, then the unarranged light
that hovers on a street before a city wakes
unrelieved to the war fumes of fuel exhaust

The city was empty, except for the three,
they seemed therefore poised, as when you are alone
anywhere all movement is arrested, light, dun,
except, their hearts, scintillant as darkness

clothy blooms of magnolia, bedraggled shrubs,
wept over a past winter, a car sped by,
scatterling from sleep, their mirage disquiets,
the subway, tumescent, expectant like a grave

They had hoped without salvation for a trolley,
they arrived at the corner impious, then,
wracked on the psalmody of the crossroad,
they felt, the absences of a morning

They circled sovereign thoughts, taking
for granted the morning, the solidity of things,
the bank to one corner, the driving school on another,
the milk store and the church

each her own separate weight,
each carried it in some drenched region of flesh,

the calculus of silence, its chaos,
the wraith and rate of absence pierced them

Chloe bathed in black, then the youngest,
leather bag strapped to a still school
girlish back, the last a precise look to her yet,
a violet lace, a hackle from forehead to neck

captured in individual doubt, a hesitation,
and what they could not put into words,
indevotion, on this eighteenth Sunday
every cool black-dressed year since 1980

This slender lacuna beguiles them,
a man frothing a biblical lexis at Christie
Pits, the small barren incline where his mad sermons
cursed bewildered subway riders, his faith unstrained

then nothing of him but his parched body's declension
a curved caesura, mangled with clippers, and
clematis cirrhosa and a budding grape vine he was still
to plant when he could, saying when he had fallen, ". . . thirsty . . ."

III

That north burnt country ran me down
to the city, mordant as it is, the whole
terror of nights with yourself and what
will happen, animus, loose like that, sweeps
you to embrace its urban meter,
the caustic piss of streets,
you surrender your heart to a numb symmetry
of procedures, you study the metaphysics of
corporate instructions and not just,
besieged by now, the ragged, serrated theories
of dreams walking by, banked in sleep

that wild waiting at traffic lights off
the end of the world, where nothing is simple,
nothing, in the city there is no simple love
or simple fidelity, the heart is slippery,
the body convulsive with disguises
abandonments, everything is emptied,
wrappers, coffee cups, discarded shoes,
trucks, street corners, shop windows, cigarette
ends, lungs, ribs, eyes, love,
the exquisite rush of nothing,
the damaged horizon of skyscraping walls,
nights insomniac with pinholes of light

IV

History doesn't enter here, life, if you call it that,
on this small street is inconsequential,
Julia, worked at testing cultures and the stingy
task, in every way irredeemable, of saving money

Then Alan came, his mother, left, came ill
squeezing a sewing machine into a hallway
and then the baby. Already you can see how
joylessness took a hold pretending to be joy

Once she had risen, reprieved from the humus subway,
heard his sermonizing, sent to her by the wind
on the harp of children and leaves and engines,
she bolted the sound of his voice pursuing

She had been expecting happiness with him, why not
a ravishing measureless happiness, he spilled instead
suspicions on her belly, where was the money
she was saving, where the light she was keeping from his hands

She would waken to find the luminous filament
of his cigarette, he rage red as the tip,
weeping, he couldn't take it any more. Then threats.
She tried tenderness. What? She must take him for a fool

The worn velvet, the late condolences
for a thing buried long before his death. Julia
sees malediction in the sly crucifix,
her back bent over specimens plotting rapture

V

That polychromatic murmur, the dizzying
waves, the noise of it, the noise of it
was the first thing. There was too
an unremitting light, through the window,
through the darkness, there was no darkness,
a steady drizzle of brightness, falling
but sleep, suddenly in the middle of it,
sleep. I woke up these mornings thinking, how
could it be rest, this clamour, but rest,
the neighbour with the vacuum cleaner and the baby
and the television's basilisk stare,
the sportscaster so sleepless,
his medicine, more noise, the fridge groaning
from the weight of ice, and the dog
wounded with absence howling downstairs

the silvery rasp of my lungs begins
to resemble everything, more engines
and stranded birds, decayed chocolate,
windscreens, my blood, a jackhammer
of breaking stars, the light again, tenacious

VI

The neighbours complained that he borrowed, took things,
rakes, saws, gloves, shovels, flowers, weeds — without asking
one tulip, three peonies, seven irises,
the devil, he said, was all in the world, abroad, he said,
his face in the quivering of baby's breath,
hold my hand, he told his daughter, the devil can't come between us

The sewing machine starting up when he left, chasing zippers,
his mother blamed her. Some proper thing Julia hadn't done,
an incantation for his un-magic life,
her good, good son had been spoiled
and there had to be blame for his distress,
hers too, threaded and buttoned between her teeth

The cornflowers, the yarrow, the lavender, the wild chamomile,
his living face in her purse. A smiling man in a double
breasted suit, his hair flared to the finger-worn corners
of the picture. He'd sent this likeness long ago to say
that he was doing well

VII

That flutter in her hand started then.
Out the door into the damp May light,
Julia looks south to the magnolia bushes,
she feels their petals in her mouth
she reaches, puts them on her tongue

she is standing on the church steps
tasting the fiction of magnolia blossoms,
another year, she had reckoned silence
might dull the meaning, it would subside
like a sentence should. But it hadn't.

She pretends fixing an imaginary seam
settling a toque on her wintry head,
she's spent her time finding things
for her runaway hand to do. All seasons.

She has become used to its rhythms,
except in public it escapes,
had she willed him to vanish? had she
a passion so hidden it happened, as passions do

tethered to this city block, this church,
these spring blossoms on her tongue,
what if she disappears into another city,

she could taste again the ordinariness of coffee
take as small but sufficient a ride on a bus
toward a named street, she could head into
her life with the same ferocity as anyone,
wake up to the pillowed hush of a snowy morning,
burrow the greyness of seven o'clock in December,
if she had not been so hasty as to get Alan killed

P. K. Page

Planet Earth: Poems Selected and New

Elegant, rigorous, fresh, P. K. Page's work sings with a voice of independent character and maenad conjecture. It is a creature that lives on its own terms and terrain. It is startling, authoritative, and anti-sentimental, able to bear cool as well as passionate gazing at our own species. Her poems are always thinking — each line is thinking, while its six senses remain impeccably alert. Her poems live by wit, wisdom, sass, suspense, and a muscular lissome synapse and diction. They are daring in scope, meticulous in accomplishment, and boldly moral — with a lovely flavour of amoral verve! We fall under the charm of her reasoning, of her fecund, fastidious imagination, of her many musics, and of her necessariness to us, her essentialness.

from ALPHABETICAL

A curious concept — *afterwards*
bearing the phantom of *before* within it.
Old-fashioned novelists fell back
on *afterwards*
to conjure up the sexual act
or when referring to religious conversion:
'afterwards her life was entirely changed.'

A shadowy comparison always implicit.

*

Before is something else. I run with it.
Before the industrial revolution
before Christ, before man
before life on this earth.
Whizzing backwards to another state.
Infinity
the ultimate destination.

Before is prelapsarian.
When I still read with care
Woolf, Maeterlinck, and Pirandello
conjurors of
the world that lay in wait —
before the metal entered, altering
the chemical components of my blood . . .

*

Who would wish carefulness on anyone?
And yet to care is vital, so, to care
to fullness should be better still.
Yet carefulness is often merely caution
a loss of nerve, the doubter's fall-back position.

*

On good days I can doubt the very floor
I stand on, even doubt the ageing flesh —
my hand, or yours.
On bad days doubt is absent and I lock
solidly into matter. Staunchly in.

*

Even. An intensive. Useful word.
To emphasize the character of something or
to indicate the unexpected or
to stress the comparative.
Even is also steady, level, flat,
without a break. Or fair
Or
balanced, even.

*

My ancestors came from the Essex fens
where winds blew in from the sea
and chilled their bones and destroyed their lungs.
They died young.
Land like a cold plate.

Alberta — flat too if you looked eastward.
I preferred the foothills, rode up from the plains
on my cayuse into the mountains.
Closer to God.

*

God. There's a subject for a book or two.
As if there aren't enough of them already.
How strange that we imagine a bearded man.
The blame can't all be laid on Blake
who painted the Ancient of Days.

Christians and Jews supplicate God the Father.
Confucius and Buddha — male.

Allah is not.

In realms like this the human comprehension
is no better than a hammer
reducing everything to a nail.

*

How easy to believe humanity is
top banana on the evolutionary tree
Ha, ha!
Ignorance and ego are a pair!
If you read Rumi you will have to think again.
Read Rumi. Think again.

*

I, I, I, I, I, I say. I. I.
I think, I talk, I walk, I this, I that.
Ignorance is the root of it, how else
imagine so narrow a vertical slot
could let in Jupiter, the god of light?
And why — come to think of it — do we see the self
as single? More like a crowded room.

*

In astrology — to which
I pay lip service while unconvinced —
sun signs and planets rule,
not parents or heads of state.

Jupiter in my Aries is
the greater fortune, crown, and thunderbolt.

I love him most
as eagle.

The young Iranian
eating falafels looked like a bird of prey
and when I asked what he did, 'Sky dive' he said.
'I ride the currents. Need it like a drug.'
I dove all the livelong night that night
on currents of air.
Kissed the eagle, beak to beak.

*

Let us consider kissing. Nothing to do with love.
Or something. Sometimes.
But not as world-wide a custom as one might suppose.
That being so
I am curious to know
what, in those unkissing cultures,
they do with their lips?

*

Love. There's another word for you. All but perished.
A concept with an inadequate label. *Love* won't do.
As many kinds as the Inuit's words for snow.
What is it you feel for your mother?
For your dog?

I once was caught in its slipstream
and like dust
in a ray of sunlight
everything shone.

Growing up on the prairie we were hooligans.

Our eastern cousins thought we had long nails
and dressed in skins. Would that we had had!
Had.

Instead we were models of propriety: gloves and
stockings in midsummer.
None but my mother
thought it was absurd.

Thirty years later travelling in New Guinea
the ladies of the administration
wore long white kid gloves to tea
a formality unheard of surely even in Court circles.

Racism or loneliness. A need to conjure
a remembered or invented past.
Dinner jackets in the jungle.

*

THE SELVES

Every other day I am an invalid.
Lie back among the pillows and white sheets
lackadaisical O lackadaisical.
Brush my hair out like a silver fan.
Allow myself to be wheeled into the sun.
Calves'-foot jelly, a mid-morning glass of port,
these I accept and rare azaleas in pots.

The nurses humour me. They call me 'dear'.
I am pilled and pillowed into another sphere
and there my illness rules us like a queen,
is absolute monarch, wears a giddy crown
and I, its humble servant at all times, am its least
serf on occasion and excluded from the feast.

Every other *other* day I am as fit
as planets circling.
I brush my hair into a golden sun,
strike roses from a bush,
rare plants in pots
blossom within the green of my eyes, I am
enviable O I am enviable.

Somewhere in between the two, a third
wishes to speak, cannot make itself heard,
stands unmoving, mute, invisible,
a bolt of lightning in its naked hand.

THE METAL AND THE FLOWER

Intractable between them grows
a garden of barbed wire and roses.
Burning briars like flames devour
their too innocent attire.
Dare they meet, blackened wire
tears the intervening air.

Trespassers have wandered through
texture of flesh and petals.
Dogs like arrows moved along
pathways that their noses knew.
While the two who laid it out
find the metal and the flower
fatal underfoot.

Black and white at midnight glows
this garden of barbed wire and roses.
Doused with darkness roses burn
coolly as a rainy moon;
beneath a rainy moon or none
silver the sheath on barb and thorn.

Change the garden, scale and plan;
wall it, make it annual.
There the briary flower grew.
There the brambled wire ran.
While they sleep the garden grows,
deepest wish annuls the will:
perfect still the wire and rose.

FUNERAL MASS

In his blackest suit
the father carries the coffin

It is light as a box of Kleenex
He carries it in one hand

It is white and gold
A jewel box

Their baby is in it

In the unconscionable weather
the father sweats and weeps

The mother leans
on the arms of two women friends

By the sacred light of the church
they are pale as gristle

The priests talk Latin
change their elaborate clothes

their mitres, copes
their stoles embroidered by nuns

Impervious to grief
their sole intention

is the intricate ritual
of returning a soul to God

this sinless homunculus
this tiny seed

Margaret Avison was born in Galt, Ontario, and raised in Regina, Calgary, and Toronto. She has won two Governor General's Awards, for her poetry collections *Winter and Sun* and *No Time*, she has been awarded three honorary doctorates, and she is a Member of the Order of Canada. Her other publications include *The Dumbfounding, sunblue, Selected Poems, A Kind of Perseverance*, and *Not Yet Still. Concrete and Wild Carrot* was published in 2002 by Brick Books.

Dionne Brand was born in Trinidad, now lives in Toronto, and lectures at York University and at Simon Fraser University in Burnaby, British Columbia. She won the Governor General's Award and the Trillium Award for her previous book of poetry, *A Land to Light On*. She is an acclaimed writer of short stories and novels, including *In Another Place Not Here, At the Full Change of the Moon*, and *Sans Souci and Other Stories*, and has directed four documentary films for the National Film Board of Canada, focusing on black women artists and activists. *Thirsty* was published in 2002 by McClelland & Stewart.

Kathleen Jamie was born in the west of Scotland, lives in Fife, and teaches Creative Writing at St. Andrews University. She has received several prestigious awards for her poetry, including the Somerset Maugham Award, a Forward Prize, and a Creative Scotland Award. She has twice won the Geoffrey Faber Memorial Prize. Her celebrated volumes, *The Queen of Sheba* and *Jizzen*, were shortlisted for both the T. S. Eliot and Forward Prizes. *Mr and Mrs Scotland Are Dead: Poems 1980–1999* was published in 2002 by Bloodaxe Books.

Paul Muldoon was born in Northern Ireland and now lives in the United States, where he is Howard G. B. Clark Professor of the Humanities and Director of the Creative Writing Program at Princeton University. In 1999 he was elected Professor of Poetry at Oxford University. He is the author of eight previous volumes of poetry, including *New Weather, Mules, Why Brownlee Left, Quoof, Meeting the British, Madoc: A Mystery, The Annals of Chile,* and *Hay. Poems 1968–1998,* published by Farrar Straus Giroux in 2001, is a collection of his eight volumes. Paul Muldoon is a Fellow of the Royal Society of Literature and the American Academy of Arts and Sciences, and has won the T. S. Eliot Prize and Irish Times Literature Prize for Poetry, among other awards. *Moy Sand and Gravel* was published in 2002 by Farrar, Straus and Giroux.

P. K. Page was born in England, raised on the Canadian prairies, and now resides in Victoria, British Columbia. She is the author of more than a dozen books, including ten volumes of poetry, a novel, selected short stories, three books for children, and a memoir, entitled *Brazilian Journal,* based on her extended stay in Brazil with her late husband Arthur Irwin, who served as the Canadian Ambassador. She has won the Governor General's Award for poetry and been appointed a Companion of the Order of Canada. A two-volume edition of Page's collected poems, *The Hidden Room,* was published in 1997. *Planet Earth: Poems Selected and New* was published in 2002 by The Porcupine's Quill.

Gerald Stern has taught at Columbia University, New York University, Sarah Lawrence College, the University of Pittsburgh, and at the Writers' Workshop at the University of Iowa, and now lives in New Jersey. He is the author of 12 previous books of poetry, most recently *Last Blue.* Among his many honours are the Lamont Prize, the National Book Award, a Guggenheim Foundation fellowship, three National Endowment of the Arts awards, a fellowship from the Academy of Arts and Letters, and the Ruth Lilly Prize. *American Sonnets: Poems* was published in 2002 by W. W. Norton.

C. D. Wright was born and raised in the Ozark Mountains of Arkansas, and is now a professor of English at Brown University. In 1994 she was named State Poet of Rhode Island. She has published nine collections of poetry, including two book-length poems, *Deepstep Come Shining* and *Just Whistle*. She is a recipient of fellowships from the Guggenheim Foundation and National Endowment for the Arts, and awards from the Foundation for Contemporary Performance Arts and the Lannan Foundation. *Steal Away: Selected and New Poems* was published in 2002 by Copper Canyon Press.

ACKNOWLEDGEMENTS

The publisher thanks the following for their kind permission to reprint the work contained in this volume:

"Inhumation," "Bosegran," "God Almighty the First Garden Made," "Arraheids," "Child with Pillar Box and Bin Bags," "Den of the Old Men," "One of Us," and "Skeins o Geese" from *Mr and Mrs Scotland Are Dead* by Kathleen Jamie are reprinted by permission of Bloodaxe Books.

"The Misfits," "Beagles," "Winter Wheat," "The Stoic," "On," "Eugenio Montale: *The Eel*," "The Ancestor," and "Homesickness" from *Moy Sand and Gravel* by Paul Muldoon are reprinted by permission of Farrar, Straus & Giroux.

"The Inkspots," "Peaches," "Mimi," "All I Did for Him," "Spider," "Hats," "Hydrangea," "Large Pots," "Samaritans," and "Roses" from *American Sonnets* by Gerald Stern are reprinted by permission of W. W. Norton.

"What No One Could Have Told Them," "The Next to Last Draft," "Song of the Gourd," "Everything Good Between Men and Women," "Ponds, In Love," and "Spring Street Girl Friend (#8)" from *Steal Away* by C. D. Wright are reprinted by permission of Copper Canyon Press.

"Present from Ted," "Ramsden," "Balancing Out," "The Whole Story," "Cycle of Community," and "Prospecting" from *Concrete and Wild Carrot* by Margaret Avison are reprinted by permission of Brick Books.

"I," "II," "III," "IV," "V," "VI," and "VII" from *thirsty* by Dionne Brand are reprinted by permission of McClelland & Stewart.

"The Selves," "The Metal and the Flower," "Funeral Mass," and the excerpt from "Alphabetical" from *Planet Earth* by P. K. Page are reprinted by permission of The Porcupine's Quill.